The Waldorf School Book of Soups

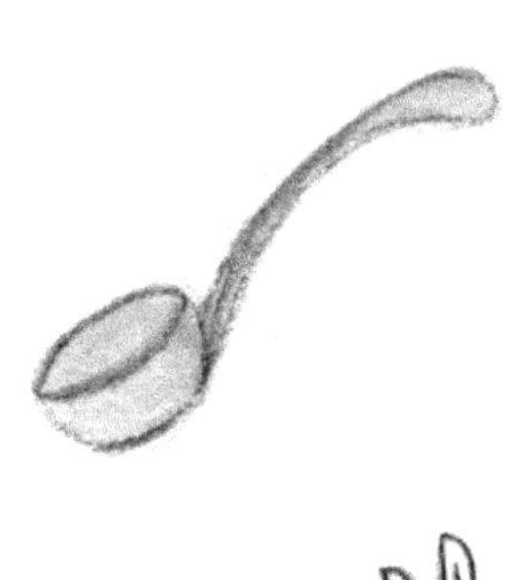

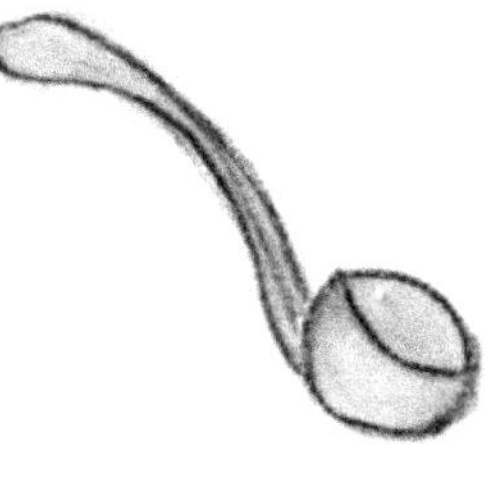

The Waldorf School Book of Soups

Collected by Marsha Post
Arranged and Introduced by Andrea Huff
Illustrated by Jo Valens

BELL POND BOOKS

Soups on p. 11 are from *the Vegan Family Cookbook* © Brian P. McCarthy
Published by Lantern Books, NY

Published by Bell Pond Books
610 Main Street
Great Barrington, Massachusetts 01230

Printed in the United States of America

Contents

Acknowledgements

Many Waldorf school teachers, parents, alumni, staff, and friends of the Waldorf movement contributed their favorite recipes for this book of soups. Some have identified themselves and the school with which they are affiliated. We will think of you as we enjoy every cup or bowl of your soup. Thank you! Others have chosen to submit their recipes anonymously. Thank you whoever you are! And special gratitude goes to Andrea Huff who arranged and introduced this book, and rounded it out by adding some of her own favorites.

Now, go have a bowl of soup!

Bell Pond Books

Abbreviations Used in this Cookbook

tsp. = teaspoon
T. = Tablespoon

Introduction

This wonderful little book is a celebration of soups from a myriad of Waldorf school communities nationwide. Since soups represent the most universally appreciated of appetizers, it gives a kind of clue to the fundamental approaches to nutrition enjoyed by so many of our friends in the families and social networks that constitute Waldorf schools in the United States. And furthermore, it represents an opportunity to sing the high praises of nutritious broths and stocks, which are an element of old-fashioned cooking that deserves re-examination and re-evaluation. Stocks and broths are the basic element from which any great soup can be created. And scientific research proves that stocks and broths can provide great nutritional benefits, in the most cost-effective ways imaginable.

A few years ago in the earliest days of this 21st century, I was shown a graph chart by a friend who works in the healing arts. The graph tracked the mineral content of the U.S. food supply from 1900 onwards. The graph indicated consistently high levels of minerals in the earliest years around 1900, then a gradual diminishment until 1975. After 1975, to the end of the 20th century, the decline in the mineral content of conventional food in the U.S. was shown to be precipitous. An opportunity to re-mineralize our bodies, and re-energize our communities through appropriate cooking, can begin with well-made stocks and broths made with natural, organic, and Bio-dynamic ingredients.

I spent my early childhood in an extended family of Italian-Americans that included grandparents from the old country, who, during the nineteen-fifties in the suburbs of Philadelphia, Pennsylvania, held sway in kitchens that represented a kind of cultural nexus and were at the heart of all family activities. We enjoyed seasonal cuisine, religious festival cuisine, holiday cooking, open house celebrations, rite-of-passage feasts, joyous entertaining of guests and relatives; and the food from those grandparents was always superb.

The most comforting and delicious, and most clearly remembered, culinary delights from those days, were for me, the delicate chicken broth, the fine beef broth, and the fabled, clear-as-a-bell fish stock produced by those talented and devoted senior cooks.

This, of course, was an era that preceded the advent of the phenomenon of fast food.

I was fortunate as a child to have been served great food prepared with high quality ingredients, and with skill and attention to detail, and with wisdom and love. As a result, I acquired taste and discretion concerning food quality. These are invaluable assets, which you too can develop and convey to your families and communities through the experience of good cooking and enjoyable eating.

Please do read the notes included in the chapter on stocks and broths, and join me in creating greater health and happiness for an ever-world-widening circle of loved ones through cookery. Don't forget to buy biodynamically, organically, and locally. Get to know and support your local farmers! Make friends with your local grocer, butcher, and fishmonger. It's a community effort.

May we succeed in tending life with proper attention.

With love,
Andrea Giambrone Huff

Stocks and Broths

Notes on Broth and Stock

Biodynamic agriculture harnesses the synergy between the various kingdoms of nature and the cosmos to produce the very valuable and effective bio-dynamic "preparations," which, when applied to compost piles or to the fields directly, bring healing to the earth and also promote fertility, eco-balance, and high product quality in the best CSA vegetable gardens, and bio-dynamic farms and vineyards throughout the world. The best gelatinous broths and stocks are products, as well, of the synergistic combinations of ingredients thoughtfully combined and prepared to enhance human digestion and to promote overall health and enjoyment.

Salty and warm, a good soup can be the primal beginning of any holistic eating experience. The basis of a densely nutritious soup or sauce is, of course, a carefully prepared stock or broth.

Although the practice of making broth and stock has largely disappeared from the American kitchen, there is growing evidence that the minerals from bone, cartilage, marrow and vegetables, and the gelatin that abounds in properly prepared broth are effective therapeutically, not only to aid basic digestion, but also to offer protective factors in the diet that can be helpful in cases of anemia, certain blood disorders, diabetes, muscular dystrophy, and cancer.

When animal tendons and cartilage are stewed into stock and broth, healing elements are put at the disposal of the human body as therapies for rheumatoid arthritis and other ailments.

Modern science has confirmed that chicken broth, long known as "Jewish penicillin," does offer protective factors against infectious diseases such as colds and flu, and can be helpful in treating asthma and other infectious diseases.

The hydrophilic colloids that broth or stock provide through gelatin attract digestive juices to the surface of foods that your body is trying to digest during a meal, and therefore are of particular use to those suffering from digestive disorders such as hyperacidity, colitis, and Crohn's disease. In general, stocks and broths, through the very valuable gelatin they provide, allow the body to maximize, through more complete digestion, whatever is ingested.

Although stewing fish heads may seem arcane to most modern Americans, the iodine, and other elements from the thyroid glands of the fish used, could provide a natural tonic for Americans, 40% of whom are reported to be suffering from thyroid gland deficiencies, the litany of symptoms of which can be listed as including:

- Fatigue
- Weight gain
- Frequent colds and flu
- Inability to concentrate
- Depression
- Heart disease
- Cancer*

For fish stock, or fish fumet, use the bones from lean flatfish like sole and turbot. Bones from salmon and tuna are too oily and would produce a too strongly flavored product. Use impeccably fresh fish bones, entire carcass and head. When including the valuable head, be sure to cut away the gills.

* *As reported by Sally Fallon in* Nourishing Traditions, *ProMotion Publishing, San Diego, CA 1995.*

They could discolor the final product and impart an off taste.

Ice fish bones overnight to extract blood, for a clearer stock.

Broth is generally regarded as being made with higher meat to bone ratio than stock, which is usually made from bonier parts of poultry, meat, or fish. Stock is often cooked for longer periods of time, and is sometimes cooked further to reduce the amount of liquid and to concentrate flavor. Very little salt is used in stock, whereas, it is often customary to accentuate the flavors in broth with small amounts of salt. The addition of a small amount of vinegar is recommended to acidify the stock or broth. This facilitates the release of minerals such as calcium, magnesium and potassium into the finished product.

In beef stock, it is considered that meat, bone, and fat in the right proportions contribute to a high quality product. Two-thirds lean meat to one third bone and fat would produce a flavorful, mineral-rich and gelatinous stock. The lean meat lends flavor and color; the bones, mineral matter and the very valuable gelatin. Fat is necessary, as it adds flavor and enhances the absorption of minerals and vitamins. Excess fat can be skimmed off the chilled, finished product, but use of some fat makes for extra deliciousness and nutrition in the soups you can creatively build from the basis of a strong stock or broth.

The making of stocks and broths is a very economical enterprise, since in all stocks or broths of animal origin, gelatin comes mainly from bones, cartilage, skin, tendons, and ligaments. Even in the case of vegetables, the use of the entire plant in the stock or broth, including the etherically loaded caps of carrots — where yin meets yang, as it were — or the minerally dense roots of leeks, will lend extra energy, vitamins, and minerals to the final soup. It is a return to the old-fashioned practice of using the whole organism, of honoring the natural gestalt, which brings a spiritual and economical integrity to digestion and to consciousness. Use bones of beef or lamb, and carcasses left from the fowl or non-oily fish you may have served; use tougher trimmings of vegetables and onion skins, etc. Of course, you can always stew a nice, whole chicken, and make a delicious salad with the meat. Aim for a gelatinous, jelly-like product. Your success in this regard is apparent after the broth or stock has been chilled. You will be bringing a health-giving benefit to all those you serve.

Large quantities of stock or broth can be reduced to concentrates, as part of a further cooking process. A reduced concentrated stock, known as glace or fumet, is a jellylike, concentrated flavor-booster, used to great effect in sauces, and to add richness to soups, stews, and other foods.

Stocks or broths made in large quantities can be stored in the refrigerator for 4 to 5 days safely. They can be stored for longer periods if brought to a boiling point, and then re-chilled. You can store broth and stock in the freezer for up to three months.

To Clarify Stock:

Remove fat from chilled stock. Put stock to be clarified into a large pot. Whisk together 1 egg white and its well-broken shell, plus two teaspoons cold water, per quart of defatted stock to be clarified. Whisk egg white, water, and shells into the pot of stock. Continue whisking, until stock reaches a boiling point. Stop whisking. Boil for about 3 minutes. Remove from heat. Let stand. Lift off the white foam crust that forms on the surface. Strain stock through a chinois or a strainer lined with dampened cheesecloth.

Vegetable Stock

For about 4 quarts of vegetable stock, start with an 8-quart stockpot. The ratio of vegetables to water is approximately 2 parts vegetables to 1 part water. Avoid long stewing of cruciferous vegetables like cabbage and broccoli, as their sulfur content can make them smelly.

Rely on the basic three: onions, carrots, and celery, as the foundation for any successful stock. Addition of other vegetables will enrich the flavor.

5-7 onions washed, but unpeeled
5-7 carrots, unpeeled
3-5 celery stalks

Add, optionally:
2-3 whole leeks
3-5 parsnips, unpeeled
2-3 kohlrabi, unpeeled
1 rutabaga, unpeeled
5 cloves garlic
1 bunch parsley
thyme, fresh (5 sprigs) or dried (1/2 tsp.)
5 black peppercorns
1 bay leaf
2 tsp. sea salt

Roughly chop vegetables. Leeks require careful washing to remove dirt, especially their roots — if they are used — and between the layers of their leaves. Put vegetables in stockpot and cover with water. Bring to a boil over high heat. Cover, lower heat, and simmer for about 40 minutes. Uncover and simmer for about 40 more minutes.

Taste stock, and if you prefer a stronger flavor, continue simmering for about 40 more minutes, uncovered.

Strain stock, cool, and refrigerate or freeze.

White Soup Stock

1 to 2 pounds marrow bones, cracked;
4 pounds veal knuckles, cracked; or 3 to 4 pounds chicken carcasses, or chicken backs and necks, wings, or legs, bones cracked with a cleaver to release their nutritious goodness while cooking; or use a combination of any of the above.

cold water, 3 quarts
2 ribs celery, chopped
1 carrot, sliced
1 onion, chopped
parsley, chopped
peppercorns
1 T. sea salt
2 T. white vinegar

Scrape marrow from bones; melt in stockpot over moderate heat. Add the rest of the bones and meat. Cover with water. Place a lid on pot and bring slowly to a boil. Remove scum. Add vinegar.

Add vegetables and seasonings. (For extra flavor, vegetables may be simmered in 2 tablespoons butter for 10 minutes before adding to soup.) Cover and simmer gently for about 4 hours; remove scum occasionally.

Strain; chill.

Makes about 2 quarts stock.

Quick Rich Chicken Broth

(This only works with a certain type of heavy, lidded enamel roaster.)

One heavy enamel roasting pan with heavy lid (Chantal brand is great)
1 organic chicken (at least 4 pounds) with giblets, (except chicken liver)
ground rosemary
sea salt
water

Separate giblets. Reserve liver for other use. Rinse heart, lungs, neck, etc. Place in bottom of roasting pan.

Rinse chicken and pat dry. Dust the skin with ground rosemary and sea salt.
Place whole chicken in roasting pan.

Add 2 to 3 inches of water to the pan. Cover. Roast at high temperature (425° to 450° F) for 1-1/2 to 2 hours. Chicken will be very tender, and you will have gelatinous broth!

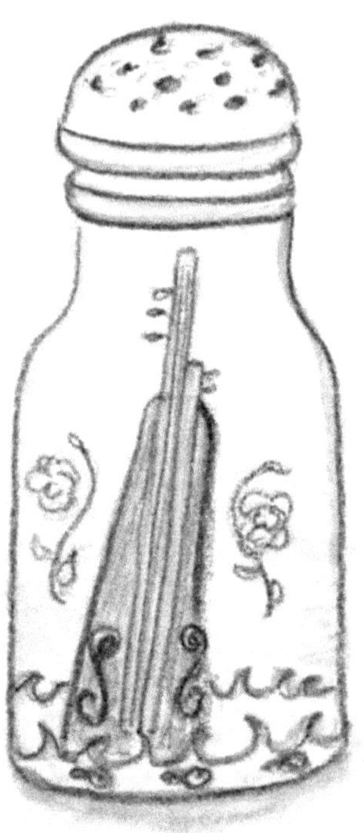

Another Quick Rich Chicken Broth

chicken backs and necks
or chicken legs
onions, chopped
butter
2 quarts boiling water
2 T. white vinegar

Using a meat cleaver, a heavy-duty chef's knife, or strong kitchen shears, cut the chicken into small pieces to release flavor. You can pound the bones a bit to prepare them to release their minerals and marrow.

Sauté onion and small chicken pieces in butter until chicken loses its raw aspect. Cover pot, and continue to simmer at low temperature (a flame-tamer, a device used to elevate the pot from the heat source, is good to use here) for about 20 minutes. Add boiling water and vinegar, and simmer, covered, for 20 to 30 minutes longer. Strain and chill.

Deep Sea Consommé

4 pounds seafood (fish bones and head, the shells and small claws from a lobster or crab or two, and a few clams, oysters, or scallops, etc.)
herb bouquet (parsley, thyme, bay)
1 onion stuck with a couple of cloves
celery leaves
1 cup white wine, or 1/4 cup white or red wine vinegar
6 cups water

Put seafood in a heavy stockpot and cover with water. Add herbs, vegetables, and wine or vinegar. Gradually bring pot to a boil, and then reduce temperature and simmer, on a low flame, for about 2 hours.

Fish Fumet

1/4 cup clarified butter
11 pounds fish bones
1/2 cup thinly sliced onions
1 thinly sliced leek
2 thinly sliced parsnips
2 thinly sliced celery ribs
1 gallon cold water
1 quart dry white wine

spice sachet including:
parsley stems
thyme
cracked black peppercorns
1 bay leaf
2 garlic cloves
pinch of sea salt (optional)

[As a preliminary: Use impeccably fresh fish bones. Remove gills from fish heads. Ice bones overnight to extract blood, which could cloud stock.]

In a shallow pan heat clarified butter, and then add the fish bones and vegetables. Sauté, or sweat, the bones and vegetables. Cover and simmer. Transfer to a stockpot and add water, wine, sachet, and optional salt. Bring to a simmer. Simmer for about 40 minutes, and skim as necessary.

Strain. Use immediately, or store for later use.

Brown Stock Varieties

Brown Chicken Stock: 8 to 9 pounds chicken bones and lean trim.

Brown Veal Stock: 8 to 9 pounds veal bones, including knuckles and trim

Brown Game Stock: 8 to 9 pounds game bones. Include juniper berries and/or fennel seeds in spice sachet.

Brown Pork Stock: (good in bean or potato soups) 8 to 9 pounds fresh or smoked pork bones. Add mustard seeds, crushed red pepper, oregano stems, or caraway seeds to spice sachet.

Brown Lamb Stock: 8 to 9 pounds lamb bones and trim. Add mint stems, juniper berries, rosemary, or cumin seeds to spice sachet.

Brown Duck Stock: 8 to 9 pounds duck bones and lean trim (or bones of other game birds, such as pheasant). Add fennel seeds and juniper berries to spice sachet.

Basic Recipe

3-4 ounces oil
8-9 pounds bones and lean trim
Rinsed and dried
6-1/2 quarts cold water

3 T. butter
1 cup onions, diced
2 carrots, diced
2 ribs celery, sliced
6-8 ounces tomato paste
Spice sachet: (parsley, thyme, cracked peppercorns, 1 bay leaf, clove of garlic)
sea salt (optional)

Pre-heat oiled roasting pan in hot (425°–450° F) oven. Add bones and trim to pan. Roast the bones about 30 to 45 minutes. Stir often during roasting process to promote even browning.

Remove bones and trim to a large stockpot. Add cool water. Use additional water to deglaze roasting pan. Add drippings to stockpot. Using low heat, slowly bring stock to a simmer. Continue to simmer gently and evenly. Skim when necessary. Simmer for about 5 hours.

In a smaller pan heat butter and sauté onions, carrots and celery. Add tomato paste and stir frequently. Add this mixture to the stock, along with spice sachet. Simmer entire stock for about 1 more hour Skim if necessary.

Strain the stock. Use immediately; or rapidly cool in an ice bath, and store.

(Based on instructions in The Professional Chef, The Culinary Institute of America, published by John Wiley & Sons, Inc., NY, 2002.)

Bean, Pea, and Lentil Soups

Barley and Bean Minestrone

2 T. olive oil
1 onion
1 stalk celery
1 small bunch parsley
1/2 lb. pearl barley
1 cup dried pinto beans, soaked overnight
2 bay leaves
1 T. tomato paste
salt and pepper

Finely chop onion, celery and parsley together. Sauté gently in olive oil. Add barley, stir well, and cover with 4 cups water. Partially cover, let come to a boil, then simmer for at least 2 hours, stirring now and then with a wooden spoon.

In the meantime, cook the beans separately in boiling water with bay leaves for the same amount of time as the barley. Add the beans and their cooking liquid to the barley, and then add the tomato paste, diluted in a little hot broth. Season with salt and pepper. Let the soup simmer for another 40 minutes. Sprinkle with grated parmesan cheese and serve in warmed bowls.

Serves 4

Anne Saldo, Enrollment Director
Westside Waldorf School
Santa Monica, CA

Chickpea, Tomato, and Pasta Soup

10 cups chicken stock
2 15-ounce cans chick peas (rinsed well)
1 28-ounce can diced tomatoes. with liquid
1-1/2 cups short pasta (bow tie, fusilli, or — my favorite — rotelli)
2 sprigs fresh rosemary
6-8 cloves garlic, roughly chopped
2 or 3 T. olive oil

In a large soup pot, heat the chicken stock to a boil; reduce heat, and add chickpeas and rosemary sprigs. Let simmer.

In another soup pot, heat the olive oil, then add the garlic. Sauté until golden. Add tomatoes (with juice). Let simmer (ten minutes or so) until flavors blend, and add to the chicken stock; let simmer for 20 minutes to 1/2 hour with lid on. Remove rosemary sprigs; using a slotted spoon, remove half the chickpeas; puree in a food processor (or blender) with some of the soup liquid. Return the puree to the soup to thicken it. Mix in well. Let simmer.

Cook the pasta in water, or chicken stock (preferable) if you have extra on hand, for 3 minutes less than the recommended time on the package, until just al dente.

Add pasta to soup. Stir well, and serve in large bowls with grated parmesan (or romano) on the side.

Serves 8-10

Loren Segan

Potato, Bean, and Bacon Soup

1/4 pound hickory-cured slab bacon, diced
2 T. bacon fat
2 T. unsalted butter
1/2 onion, diced
1 rib celery, diced
1 carrot, diced
4 cups chicken stock
salt and pepper to taste
2 leeks, washed and cut into 1/2-inch circles
2 potatoes, peeled and cubed
1/2 large red pepper, diced
10-1/2 oz. can great northern beans

In a large pot boil bacon for 5 minutes. Drain on paper towel. Dry pan, put bacon back in and fry for 4 minutes until crisp. Remove and drain all fat except 2 T. Add butter, onions, carrots and celery and sauté for 5 minutes. Skim off fat. Add leeks and potatoes. Simmer for 5 minutes.

Add pepper. Simmer until potatoes are tender. Add beans. Heat through.

Serves 4-6

Byron Shepard, Grandparent
Pleasant Ridge Waldorf School
Viroqua, WI

Tuscan White Bean Soup in the Slow Cooker

This recipe is basic and can be adjusted in any way you wish. The extra virgin olive oil is important. I like to cook the soup overnight then refrigerate it for a day. I then serve it that evening for more flavor.

1 cup onion, diced and sautéed in olive oil until soft
1 red or yellow pepper, diced
2 stalks celery, diced
2 small zucchini in small pieces
1 T. herbs de Provence or other herbs, crushed
1 large can white or other type beans, drained *or* 1 pound dried white beans, soaked and drained
grated Parmigiano Reggiano cheese for garnish

Put in slow cooker with 3 to 4 fresh chopped tomatoes or a large can of whole tomatoes squeezed by hand. Add 6 to 8 cups of liquid to cooker — water, chicken broth, vegetable broth or a combination.

Add the beans to the pot. Add 2 to 3 T. of extra virgin olive oil, herbs de Provence, or other herbs of choice. Cook 8 hours on high in slow cooker.

Drizzle with olive oil and sprinkle generously with grated Parmigiano Reggiano cheese and serve.

Sweet Italian sausage or other meats may be cooked and added before serving.

Serves 6-8

Peg Savage, Staff Member
Kimberton Waldorf School

Adzuki and Peanut Soup

1 cup dried adzuki beans, rinsed
4 cups water
2 carrots, diced
3 ribs celery, diced
1/2 onion, diced
1 bell pepper, diced
1/4 cup light olive oil
1/2 cup flour
1 garlic clove
1 tsp. thyme
1/4 tsp. black pepper
4 cups vegetable broth
salt to taste
1-1/2 cups roasted peanuts

Combine water with beans in a stock pot. Bring to a boil, reduce heat and simmer for 1 hour, or until beans are tender. Drain off the water and set beans aside.

In a large pot, sauté the garlic, and then the carrots, celery, onion, and bell pepper in the oil, until the vegetables are tender. Reduce heat to low. Add the flour, thyme, and black pepper, and continue to sauté for 2 minutes. Add the vegetable broth and the reserved cooked beans. Heat soup on medium/high heat until thickened, stirring often. Add salt to taste.

Sprinkle peanuts on top right before serving.

Serves 6

Brian P. McCarthy, from
The Vegan Family Cookbook

Minestrone Soup

2 carrots, diced
3 ribs celery, diced
1/2 onion, diced
3 T. light olive oil
4 cups vegetable broth
1/2 cup uncooked elbow pasta
1/2 bunch spinach, chopped
1 15-oz. can diced or crushed tomatoes
1 15-oz. can kidney beans (or a varitey of beans), drained and rinsed
1-1/2 tsp. basil
1 tsp. oregano
garlic (optional)
salt to taste

In a large pot, sauté the carrots, celery, onion, and garlic in the oil until tender. Add vegetable broth, pasta, spinach, beans, basil, and oregano. Bring to a boil, stirring often. Reduce heat to low and cover. Let simmer for 15 minutes or until pasta is cooked, stirring occasionally. Add salt to taste.

Serves 6

Brian P. McCarthy, from
The Vegan Family Cookbook

Bubbe's Split Pea Soup with Dumplings (Treiflach)

I learned how to make this wonderful, healthful and body warming soup from my mother-in-law, Clara Geller. It is one of my favorites, and "Bubbe" (Yiddish for Grandma) used to make it often. I have made it for some people here in Viroqua, and everyone has loved it so far. The word "Trieflach" is Yiddish and comes from the German "triefen," to drip, which simply means that the dumplings are not rolled in your hands but rather dropped from the side of a spoon. Just don't let the word "drip" fool you, though. The dough mustn't be runny and actually "drip" from the spoon. It has to be a little firmer so that you can "drop" it into the boiling soup. I wish Bubbe were still around to show you that part.

Soup:

1 pound green split peas, rinsed (I've never used yel1ow peas, but you could try them)
6-8 cups water *or* beef broth *or* vegetable broth *or* a mix of water and broth, more if needed
2-3 whole onions, peeled
3-5 carrots, depending on size, cut into 1-inch chunks
2 stalks celery, cut into 1-inch chunks
salt and pepper to taste
1/2 tsp. dried dill, or more to taste, *or* 1 T. fresh dill
2 T. butter (optional)
smoked ham, cubed (optional)

Dumplings:

2 large eggs
1/2 cup plus 1 T. flour
Pinch of salt
Pinch of dill (optional)

Put 6 cups water and/or broth and the split peas into a 6-8 qt. heavy-bottomed (to prevent scorching) stockpot. Bring to a boil and add whole onions. Let cook for about 30 minutes on medium heat. Add carrots and celery and simmer for another 45 to 60 minutes or until soup begins to thicken. Make sure the peas don't stick at the bottom. Stir frequently. Add the remaining 2 cups broth as needed to prevent sticking. Use more liquid if you desire a thinner soup. Add a little salt, pepper, and the dill.

In the meantime, lightly beat the eggs; and then add the flour gradually, mixing with a fork or a small whisk until all lumps are gone and the mixture is shiny, but not runny. You will definitely need the 1/2 cup of flour. Whether you will need more or not depends on the size of the eggs. Don't make the dough too dry either, or the dumplings will become hard. When the soup has the desired thickness (personal preference), turn the heat up to medium high so that the soup bubbles. With the side of a tablespoon scoop up some of the batter (to fill only the long edge of the spoon, perhaps 1/2 inch) and insert it near the wall of the pot (that's where the soup is hottest). The batter will fall off the spoon, and you continue with the remainder, going around the edge of the pot. Keep the soup bubbling gently without burning it. As soon as all of the batter is swimming in the soup, put a tight-fitting lid on the pot, turn down the heat and let it simmer until all of the dumplings have risen to the top and are nicely plump.

If desired, round out the flavor with 2 to 3 T. butter at the very end. (Add ham — optional.) Adjust seasonings and enjoy.

Served with fresh, crusty bread and a salad, this soup can be a main dish for 4 people. It's delicious as a leftover and can be frozen.

Serves 4-6

Malkah Geller, German Language Mentor
Pleasant Ridge Waldorf School
Viroqua, Wisconsin

Split Pea with Sweet Potato Soup

1 lb. green split peas
2-3 quarts chicken broth
4 large carrots, coarsely chopped
1 large onion, chopped
1 large sweet potato, peeled and chopped
2 stalks celery, chopped
1-1/2 T. butter
1 tsp. basil
1 clove garlic, minced
1/2 tsp. ground cumin
1/2 cup dry white wine (optional)
peppercorns or freshly ground pepper to taste
salt to taste

Combine the peas, broth, and salt in a large pot. Bring to a boil. Reduce the heat and simmer for 1 hour.

Sauté the vegetables for 5 minutes, stirring frequently. Add the herbs and simmer for an additional 5 minutes. Add this to the soup and simmer for 45 minutes.

Ladle out and purée about 1/2 of the soup in a blender. (As it is impossible to purée the whole half at one time, I do part, add it back in, and repeat this until the soup has the creamy texture I want.) Return the purée to the soup mixture and add the pepper and optional wine.

The sweet potato is the secret, as it thickens the soup and sweetens it slightly.

Serves 6-8

Lynn Fitzgerald
Table Grove, IL

Ham and Bean Soup

1 pound white navy beans
1-1/2 pounds meaty ham hocks (smoked)
1 tsp. baking soda
cider vinegar

Rinse the navy beans well. Then put them in a large pot, add the teaspoon of soda, and cover them with water. Bring to a boil and remove from the heat. Drain them and rinse them again. Add ham hocks and a little salt. I also add a little sugar to bring out the flavor. Cover the ham and beans with water. Cook until the beans are soft. You can then take the ham hocks out, pull the meat off, and put the meat back into the soup. Season with salt and pepper to taste. A little vinegar may be added separately by those wanting a little zest in their soup.

Serve with fresh baked cornbread.

Serves 5-7

Velma Post
Rushville, Illinois

Rosemary Red Soup

This is a warm, yummy soup with a beautiful color. Perfect for a crisp fall night!

3 medium carrots
2 beets
1 T. extra-virgin olive oil
1 large onion, diced
2 T. fresh rosemary (or 2 tsp. dried)
1 T. fresh oregano (or 1 tsp. dried)
1 cup dried red lentils
2 bay leaves
6 cups water or stock
2-3 T. light miso

Scrub and chop carrots and beets. Heat oil in a soup pot. Add onion and sauté until soft. Add carrots and beets. Sauté a few minutes more. Finely chop rosemary and oregano leaves, if using fresh herbs. Wash and drain lentils. Add herbs, lentils, bay leaves, and water or stock to onion mix. Bring to a boil. Lower heat and simmer 40 minutes. Remove bay leaves. Puree soup in blender or processor. Dissolve miso in 1/2 cup water and add to soup. Gently reheat before serving.

Serves 6-8

Susan Townsley, Parent
Pleasant Ridge Waldorf School
Viroqua, WI

Lentil-Vegetable Soup

1-1/2 cups lentils
1/4 cup brown rice (optional)
2 cups canned crushed tomatoes
1 large onion, chopped
2-1/2 T. olive oil
3 T. fresh or 1 T. dried parsley
1 bay leaf
1 tsp. oregano
1 tsp. basil
1/2 tsp. black pepper
1 large carrot, chopped
1 large rib celery, chopped
grated cheddar cheese

Bring 6 cups of water to a boil. Add lentils and brown rice. Return to boil and add tomatoes, onion, oil, and spices. Cover and simmer 30 minutes, stirring occasionally. Add carrot and celery, and simmer, partially covered, until vegetables are tender, about 30 minutes. Stir frequently.

Serve piping hot, topped with cheddar cheese.

Serves 4 to 6

Ruth Kittleson, Alumni Parent
Pleasant Ridge Waldorf School
Viroqua. WI

Cream Soups

Celery Root and Wild Rice Soup

This soup has been served at the Youth Initiative High School's Valentine's Day Dinner.

2 celery roots, about 2 lbs.
4 large leeks
4 T. unsalted butter
2 celery ribs, diced
2 cups red potato, thinly sliced
1/2 cup parsley, chopped, plus extra for garnish
2 bay leaves
2 tsp. thyme
Celtic sea salt
2 tsp. pepper
4 cups vegetable or chicken stock *or* water
4 cups half & half *or* part milk and heavy cream
1 cup wild rice

Cook the wild rice. Cut away the celery root skins, then quarter and chop the root into bite-sized pieces. Chop and wash the leeks. Melt the butter in the soup pot. Add the vegetables, parsley, bay leaves, thyme, and 3 tsp. salt. Cook over medium high heat for 5 minutes. Add the stock and bring to a boil. Simmer for 20 minutes. Add the half & half and simmer until vegetables are tender, about 10 more minutes. Taste for salt and pepper. Puree the soup well. If it is too thick, it can be thinned with the rice water later.

Cooking the rice:

1 cup wild rice
5 cups water
pinch sea salt

Bring water to a boil. Add sea salt. Add the rice and simmer the rice for 45 minutes or until tender.

When ready to serve, heat soup gently until hot; do not boil. Ladle 1/2 cup soup per bowl and place a tablespoon of wild rice in each bowl. Sprinkle with parsley.

Serves 12-20

Jane Siemon, Alumni Parent
Pleasant Ridge Waldorf School
Viroqua, WI

Cream of Kohlrabi and Carrot Soup

1 onion, chopped
3 cloves garlic, minced
1/4 cup butter
4 or 5 kohlrabi roots, peeled and chopped
4 carrots, sliced
sea salt and white pepper
3 cups chicken broth
1 cup heavy cream
dash of cayenne
chopped cilantro *or* parsley for garnish

Sauté onion and garlic in the butter. Add carrots, and stir. Add kohlrabi and broth. Simmer for about 30 minutes, or until vegetables are tender. Process in blender or food processor until smooth. Add seasonings to taste. Heat through and add cream. Serve hot, with garnish.

Serves 4

Andrea Huff
Sheltering Arms Family Center (Waldorf Early Childhood and Parent Education Programs)
Kimberton, PA

Cream of Broccoli with Dulse Soup

2 T. butter
2 leeks, cleaned and sliced
2 heads broccoli
1 medium potato
4 cups chicken or vegetable stock (can be part water)
1/2-1 cup cream or buttermilk
1 tsp. Celtic sea salt
1 tsp. dulse, chopped
1/4 tsp. black pepper
parmesan cheese, finely grated (optional)

In a soup pot, melt the butter and add the leek and garlic. Sauté gently until soft. Wash and chop the tops off. Peel the stems and chop the core of the stems. Wash the potato and peel. Cut into 1/2-inch cubes. Put the broccoli and potato in with the leek and garlic. Add the broth and dulse. Simmer until all is tender, about 15 minutes.

Puree in a food processor or with a hand held blender. Add salt and pepper to taste. Keep hot, but not boiling.

Add the cream or buttermilk just before serving. Garnish with a sprinkling of parmesan cheese.

Serves 6

Jane Siemon, Alumni Parent
Pleasant Ridge Waldorf School
Viroqua, WI

Cream of Broccoli Soup

1/4 cup butter
1/2 cup chopped onion
1 minced garlic clove
3-1/2 cup chopped broccoli (preferably fresh)
1 tsp. lemon juice
1 cup light cream or half & half
milk
salt and pepper

Melt butter in large saucepan. Saute onion and garlic until onion is tender; add broccoli, lemon juice and 1 cup water. Cover and simmer until broccoli is tender.

Puree in blender, food processor or via vigorous stirring. Stir in cream or half & half and enough milk to bring soup to your desired consistency. Season with salt and pepper and gently re-heat.

Serves 4

Linda Finigan, Alumni Parent
Cape Ann Waldorf School
Beverly, MA

Tomato Soups

Fire Roasted Tomato Soup

2 28-ounce cans Muir Glen Organic Fire Roasted tomatoes
1/2 cup cucumber, peeled, seeded, and diced (I always cut the whole cuke)
3 T. olive oil
1/2 cup yellow onion, finely chopped
3 cloves garlic, minced
1/4 cup orange juice
1 large red bell pepper, membrane removed, finely chopped
1 T. kosher salt
1/4 tsp. fresh ground black pepper
1/4 tsp. hot pepper sauce, such as Tabasco
1 T. fresh parsley, minced
1/4 cup heavy cream
2-4 oz. aged manchego cheese, very thinly sliced

Make the soup:

In a blender, add the tomatoes and 1/4 cup cucumber and puree until smooth. Set aside. In a large saucepan, over medium-high heat, heat the olive oil. Add the onion and cook until translucent, about 4 minutes.

Reduce the heat to medium, stir in the garlic, and cook for 2 minutes.

Slowly add pureed tomato mixture, orange juice, bell pepper, salt, and black pepper and stir to combine. Continue to cook for 35 minutes.

Remove from heat and stir in the hot sauce, parsley, and cream. Serve hot, garnished with the cheese and remaining diced cucumber.

Serves 8

Penny Guy, Parent
Shepherd Valley Waldorf School
Niwot, Colorado

Fresh Tomato Soup

3 medium or 1 large onion, chopped,
or 3-4 large shallots, minced
4 medium or 2 large garlic cloves, minced
3-4 T. olive oil plus additional for flavoring
5 lbs. very ripe, fresh tomatoes (not canned)
salt
freshly ground pepper
large pinch dried oregano or marjoram or a small sprig of fresh basil
1 T. balsamic or other mild vinegar, *or* to taste (optional)
pinch sugar (optional)

In a large, non-aluminum saucepan or stockpot, sauté onion or shallots and garlic in olive oil until soft and translucent, about 7 to 8 minutes. Cut unpeeled tomatoes into quarters or eighths straight into the pot. Cover and simmer over low to medium heat until the tomatoes begin to give off their juice, about 5 minutes. Raise heat slightly and continue to simmer, stirring occasionally, until the tomatoes are completely soft and swimming in their own juice. Depending on the quantity and how crowded your pot is, this process may take from 15 to 45 minutes.

Put the soup through a food mill (watch out for splutters of sauce). Force through as much of the tomato mixture as you can. (Alternatively, the tomatoes can be pureed in batches in a food processor, but the texture will not be as good.) Return the pureed tomatoes to the pot, and return it to a simmer. Season to taste with salt, pepper, oregano, or marjoram, or if you prefer, fresh basil. Simmer for 5 to 10 minutes to amalgamate the flavors, and taste again. If it is bland, add balsamic vinegar or other mild, rich-tasting vinegar. If you must, take off any acidic edge with just a pinch of sugar, and whisk in another 1 to 2 T. olive oil just before serving.

Makes 2 quarts (6-8 servings).

Linda Gambrell, Alumni Parent
Pleasant Ridge Waldorf School
Viroqua, WI

Stale Bread and Tomato Soup

My husband's aunt is a stellar cook. She made this soup for me the first time I visited her home in NYC. Visiting NYC and eating this soup were both firsts for me at 24. I had grown up eating canned soup, white bread and lots of snack cakes and potato chips. The soup seemed so exotic to me then, as did NYC. Little did I know then that this was my first recipe in a long collection of simple meals.

5 T. olive oil
1 onion, sliced thinly
1-1/2 to 2 cups tomatoes, peeled and chopped
6-ounce can tomato paste
7 cups water
4 cups chicken broth
1 loaf stale Italian bread (not sourdough) torn into pieces
3 large cloves garlic, finely chopped
2 tsp. kosher or coarse salt
2 T. dried basil or 1/4 cup packed, fresh
salt and pepper (freshly ground) to taste
olive oil
parmesan cheese

Sauté onion in olive oil. Cook over medium heat, stirring often, until onions are soft. Add tomatoes and tomato paste, and continue to cook over low heat, stirring often, for about 15 minutes. Combine and heat the water, chicken broth, bits of bread, garlic, salt and basil in separate pot. Bring the soup and bread mixture to a simmer and cook for about 5 minutes. Then combine the tomato mixture and the soup and bread mixture in a very large pot; stir over low heat until thoroughly blended. Put soup through a food processor or puree with a hand blender. The soup can be pureed thoroughly or left with some texture. Reheat. Serve with freshly ground salt and pepper to taste, drizzle with olive oil and sprinkle with parmesan cheese.

Serves 8-10

Lisa White
Sarasota Waldorf School

Cream of Tomato Soup

1 onion, chopped
3 cloves garlic, chopped
a good knob of butter (half a stick or more)
1 28-ounce can organic tomato puree
sea salt
white pepper
cayenne
1 tsp. dried basil or 1/2 tsp. oregano
2-1/2 cups good chicken broth
2/3 cup heavy cream

Sauté onion and garlic in butter. Add tomato puree; stir and heat. Add herbs. Add chicken broth, and simmer. Add sea salt and seasoning. Simmer for 30 to 45 minutes. Add heavy cream. Check for salt and seasoning. If necessary, add more butter. Serve hot.

This soup can be used as a pasta sauce with delicious results.

Serves 4-6

Andrea Huff
Sheltering Arms Family Center
Waldorf Early Childhood and Parent Education Programs
Kimberton, PA

Vegetable Soups

Butternut Squash Soup

dash olive oil
4 cloves garlic, roughly chopped
2 medium red onions, chopped
2 medium butternut squash, peeled and chopped into chunks
4 heaped tsp. vegetable stock powder
pinch or two cinnamon
pinch or two ground ginger
salt and pepper to taste
water
sprig rosemary

In a large saucepan over a medium heat, warm olive oil. Add garlic and onion. Sauté. Add squash. Add spices and stock powder. Cover with water; place rosemary in pot. Bring to boil and simmer until squash is easily pierced with a knife. Remove rosemary and ladle into blender. Blend and serve.

Serves 6 easily, but can be thinned out to accommodate more.

Danica Wyber-Thomas, Class of 2000
Toronto Waldorf School

Easy Curry Squash Soup

This is an easy recipe, and it is good for the soul.

butternut squash cut into large, bite-size pieces with skin on
1 onion
2 cloves garlic
1 can coconut milk
2-3 T. honey
2-3 T. curry
2 tsp. salt (or to taste)
fresh cilantro, if wanted, finely chopped

Cut squash and put in pot with onion and garlic. Barely cover with water — maybe 3 to 4-1/2 inches from top of veggies. Cover and cook on medium heat 10 to 15 minutes until tender. Mix with hand blender (or put in blender) then add the rest of the ingredients and mix with hand held blender again. Add cilantro and serve.

Serves 4

Susan Schneeburg, Parent
Pleasant Ridge Waldorf School
Viroqua, WI

Classic Italian Escarole

I am a member of Threshold Farm's CSA (community supported agriculture). When my farm share includes escarole, I dig out my mother's classic recipe and invite my friends over for a real treat.

4 T. olive oil
1 large onion, chopped
4 cloves garlic, minced
2 turnips, diced
3 tomatoes, peeled and chopped
1 cup precooked (or canned) white beams
2 quarts water
1 head escarole, chopped
Salt and pepper

In a soup pot, sauté onions and garlic until the onions become clear. Add turnips and cook for 5 minutes over medium heat. Add water, beans, tomatoes, and escarole and bring to a boil. Add salt and pepper to taste. Cook 35 minutes over medium heat.

A sprinkle of Parmesan cheese dresses it up nicely.

Serves 5-6

Gloria Kemp, Retired Teacher
Hawthorne Valley School
Rudolf Steiner School, NYC

Brussel Sprout Soup

Wednesdays were Brussel Sprout Soup Days at a little diner on Washington Square Park in New York City where I spent my graduate school years at NYU. The cook would never share his recipe, but I experimented until I got it, or something very close. I think the leeks brought it close to perfection. Here it is. Enjoy.

1 pound brussel sprouts, quartered
2 medium potatoes, cubed
1 medium onion, diced
2 leeks, finely chopped
3 T. olive oil
3 bouillon cubes (vegetable or chicken)
salt and pepper to taste
2 quarts water

In a soup pot, sauté onions and leeks in olive oil until they are clear. In a small bowl, add a little of the water to the bouillon cubes and stir until they dissolve. Add this with the remaining water, brussel sprouts, and potatoes to the pot. Cook over medium heat for 40 minutes. Add salt and pepper to taste.

This soup is nice with a sprinkle of grated romano cheese on the top.

Serves 5-6

Gloria Kemp, Retired Teacher
Hawthorne Valley School
Rudolf Steiner School, NYC

Vegetable Soup I

(The secret is the butter). This was our soup when I was a kindergarten teacher at Prairie Hill Waldorf School in Pewaukee, Wisconsin. The children ate bowl after bowl, and colleagues looked forward to the possibility of leftovers!

1 regular-sized bag organic carrots
2 medium-sized organic onions
6 medium-sized organic white or red potatoes
1 12-ounce bag frozen organic peas or equal amount of fresh green beans or any other vegetables you wish to add or to replace the above listed ones
1 stick organic, lightly salted butter

Peel and chop the ingredients into the soup pot. I always peeled the carrots even though they were organic because the children loved eating the peels. Green beans are nice for snapping. Add enough water to barely cover all the ingredients, and add the butter. Cook on stovetop for 1 to 3 hours, depending upon how soft you want the vegetables to be. Bring to a boil, and then turn down to low.

Serves up to 16-20 children and 2 adults.

Cynthia Aldinger
LifeWays North America
Norman, OK

Vegetable Soup II

2 quarts good broth or water
1/2 cup barley or rice
3-1/2 T. butter
1 cup zucchini, shredded
3 onions, chopped
1/4 head cabbage, shredded
4 medium carrots
1 cup parsley and/or chives
3 celery stalks
2-4 potatoes, chopped
4 cups tomato juice
1 cup corn
1/4 cup green beans
salt and pepper

Bring broth to a boil. Add barley and cook until done (about 1/2 hour). Add salt and pepper. Sauté onions in 3-1/2 T. butter for about 5 minutes. Add carrots, celery, and potatoes. Sauté another 5 to 10 minutes and add to soup. Then add corn, green beans, zucchini, and cabbage. Bring to a boil. Cover and simmer until vegetables are done. Add tomato juice and parsley.

Serves 8-10

Mary Kehoe, Parent
Pleasant Ridge Waldorf School
Viroqua, WI

Hungarian Asparagus Soup

1 medium turnip
1 medium carrot
1 medium onion
1 pound fresh asparagus (firm)
1 bay leaf
1/2 tsp. dried marjoram
6 cups water or chicken stock
1 T. vegetable seasoning salt
1-1/2 T. unsalted butter (extra-virgin olive oil may be used instead)
2 T. whole wheat flour
salt and white pepper to taste

Wash and cut the turnip and carrot into large pieces, and chop the onion. After washing the asparagus, cut off the tips and set aside. Cut the stems into several pieces.

Combine the turnip, carrot, onion, bay leaf, marjoram, vegetable seasoning salt, and the water or stock in a large stockpot. Bring to a boil, lower the heat, cover, and simmer for 40 minutes, or until the vegetables are tender.

Purée the soup (in batches is suggested) until a creamy consistency. Strain to remove any asparagus strings, and pour back into the stockpot.

In a small skillet, heat the butter (or olive oil). Add the flour and cook 4 to 5 minutes, stirring continuously. The mixture will give off a nutty fragrance when ready. Add a bit of the soup to the skillet and stir until thoroughly combined. Pour this mixture back into the soup. Simmer the soup for 10 minutes.

Season to taste, and add the asparagus tips. Simmer 3 to 4 minutes longer.

Serves 6-8

Anonymous

Minestrone

2 T. olive oil
2 cups onion, chopped
5 medium cloves garlic, minced
1-1/2 tsp. salt
1 stalk celery, minced
1 medium carrot, diced
1 tsp. oregano
1 tsp. basil
1 medium bell pepper, diced
1 small zucchini, diced
3-4 cups water (may be more)
2 cups tomato purée
1 to 1-1/2 cups chick peas or kidney beans, already cooked
1/2 to 1 cup pasta (any shape)
1-2 medium tomatoes, diced
1/2 cup fresh parsley, minced
parmesan cheese

Heat the olive oil in a large pot. Add the onion, garlic, and salt, and sauté for about 5 minutes over medium heat. Add the celery, carrot, oregano, basil, and black pepper (black pepper, optional, to taste), and cook over low heat about 10 minutes. Stir occasionally.

Add to this the bell pepper, zucchini, tomato purée, and water. Let simmer 15 minutes. Add the cooked beans, and simmer 5 minutes more.

Bring the soup to a boil, add the pasta, and cook until the pasta is the consistency wished.
Stir in diced fresh tomatoes, top with parmesan and parsley. Serve immediately.

Serves 6-8

Anonymous

Shape Soup

3 cups broth
6-8 pieces cooked lasagna noodles
carrots cut into rounds and lightly steamed
fresh or frozen peas, lightly steamed
small cookie cutters of various shapes

Heat broth and keep at low simmer. Lay the cooked lasagna noodles out flat on a cutting board. Cut the noodles into desired shapes. We have used geometric shapes, teddy bears, stars and hearts. Add cut shapes to the broth. Add steamed vegetables. Serve.

The recipe is only limited by your imagination. We use different themes for different holidays. It has also become a family activity to look for new and unusual small cookie cutters. Zucchini, potato, eggplant, tomato casing, and cabbage also lend themselves to cutting into shapes.

Serves 4

Judy Penski and Hannah Hope Rose
Washington Waldorf School

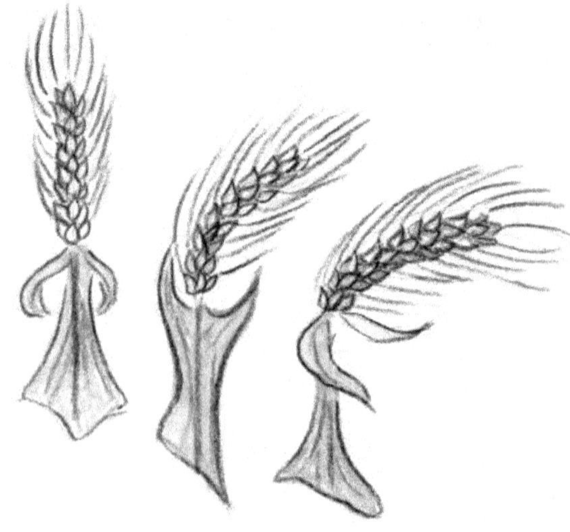

Vegetable Barley Soup

1-2 T. of oil
2-3 sticks celery
1-2 medium onions
2 cloves garlic
about 2 quarts water
1 cup barley
1 tsp. salt
1 tsp. Italian seasoning
1-2 tsp. tamari
3-4 potatoes
3- 4 carrots (winter squash is good too!)

In a large soup pot, sauté onions, celery and garlic in oil. Add water, barley, salt, Italian seasoning, and tamari. Bring to a boil and continue to boil gently for 30 minutes. Meanwhile, peel potatoes and carrots (and winter squash). Add vegetables to soup and continue gentle boil for an hour or until barley is tender. Enjoy!

Serves 8

Early Childhood Department
Cincinnati Waldorf School

Yellow Bell Pepper and Summer Squash Soup

1 large onion, chopped
1/4 cup butter
1 large yellow bell pepper, sliced
3 cups summer squash, sliced thinly
2 cloves garlic, minced
1 cup good broth
cilantro, chopped
sea salt and pepper

In a thick bottomed pot, sauté onion and garlic. Add pepper and cook, covered, about 5 minutes. Add squash; cook 10 minutes more. Stir in broth and simmer. Add salt and pepper.

In food processor or blender, puree until smooth. Return to soup pot and heat through. Adjust thickness with hot broth. Taste for seasonings. Garnish with chopped cilantro.

Makes about three cups. Serves 4

Andrea Huff
Sheltering Arms Family Center
(Waldorf Early Childhood and Parent Education Programs)
Kimberton, PA

Simply Borscht

I love borscht and have seen many recipes over the years. But when you have really tasty fresh beets from your own garden or your CSA (community supported agriculture), simplicity is best to allow the beety flavor to shine through. So here is a simple and delicious version of this popular soup. I think it actually tastes better upon reheating the next day, so I always make plenty to enjoy for several days.

3 cups beets, cubed
3 carrots, sliced
2 potatoes, cubed
½ head cabbage, finely chopped
1 onion, minced
1 can tomato paste
4 quarts water
3 T. olive oil
2 T. apple cider vinegar
1 bay leaf
salt and pepper
sour cream
dill leaves

In a soup pot, sauté onions in olive oil. Add water, beets, carrots, potatoes, cabbage, tomato paste and bay leaf. Bring to a boil. Add apple cider vinegar and salt and pepper to taste. Cook on medium heat for about 30 minutes. Remove bay leaf.

Serve with a dollop of sour cream and a sprinkle of dill.

Serves 10-12

Gloria Kemp, Retired Teacher
Hawthorne Valley School
Rudolf Steiner School, NYC

Leftovers Soup

If you are lucky enough to have some leftover spaghetti sauce (about 1 quart) and some fresh, uncooked vegetables in your refrigerator, you can make a wonderful Italian vegetable, bean, and pasta soup.

1 quart spaghetti sauce
1 to 1-1/2 quarts chicken broth
1 28-ounce can of chopped or diced tomatoes
1 15-ounce can garbanzo beans, undrained (white beans may be substituted)
Leftover pasta or small shells
pesto
parmesan
vegetable possibilities: broccoli, green beans, carrots, red peppers, onion, zucchini, celery

Combine the spaghetti sauce, broth, and diced tomatoes. Add the vegetables and cook until the vegetables are done to your liking. Add the beans and cooked pasta, and warm through. (If using uncooked pasta, add when the vegetables are almost done.)

Serve with a teaspoon of pesto and some parmesan on top.

Serves 4-6

Lynn Fitzgerald
Table Grove, IL

Easy Miso Soup

A Simple Soup for Grounding Kids

Miso is a very yang food. It is especially good for balancing diets that lean towards sweet and processed foods, which are generally yin. I make this up at least once a week, or more around the holidays, or at times of travel, or whenever my family is getting off balance...

8 ounces buckwheat or other Asian noodles *or* 2 cups cooked rice
4 cups water or stock
3 pea-sized portions tofu* for each person
2 carrots, chopped
1 cup greens, chopped
2-4 T. red miso

Optional ingredients:

2-inch dried kombu and/or wakame sea vegetables
dried shiitake mushrooms
green onions for garnish

Prepare noodles if you are using them. Bring next 4 ingredients to a boil, reduce temperature, and simmer until carrots are desired tenderness. (If using meat, make sure it is cooked through.) Turn off heat and pour a small amount of broth into a bowl. Mix in miso until smooth. Add diluted miso to pot of broth. Let stand, or carefully simmer, but do not boil. Place noodles or rice into serving bowls and ladle the soup on top. Miso is a living food — it is important that it not be boiled or it will lose some of its benefits.

**Tofu is extremely cooling, and like other unfermented soy products, should be used with caution.*

Serves 4

Melanie Nieniczura
Antioch New England Graduate School
Keene, NH

Cauliflower and Roquefort Soup

4 T. butter
1 medium onion, chopped
1 medium cauliflower
1 large potato, peeled and diced
1 quart good broth
2 T. snipped chives
A few drops of Tabasco
1 cup heavy cream
2 egg yolks, room temperature
1/2 pound roquefort cheese, crumbled
chives for garnish

Melt butter in large Dutch oven, or other large heavy-bottomed stock pot. Over moderately high heat, sauté onion for 1 minute. Add cauliflower and potato to pot and cook, stirring 1 minute. Add broth, chives, and Tabasco. Bring to a boil. Cover. Lower heat. Simmer 10 minutes, or until vegetables are just tender. Cool slightly. Puree mixture in food processor. Return to pot.

In a small bowl, blend cream and egg yolks. Add 1 cup hot soup to bowl, and whisk with wire whip. Return to pot. Add cheese. Heat very slowly, stirring constantly, until cheese melts and soup thickens slightly; do not allow it to boil. Garnish with reserved chives.

Serves 4

Beth Woodward, Parent
Cape Ann Waldorf School
Beverly, MA

First Pot of Soup Ever

1 leek, washed thoroughly and diced
4 cloves garlic, minced
2 large carrots, diced
2 to 3 Yukon gold potatoes, diced
1 head of escarole
chicken, cooked and diced
1 can of diced tomatoes
8 cups organic broth
1/4 tsp. thyme
1 bay leaf
1/2 tsp. salt

Sauté leeks and minced garlic in small amount of vegetable oil. Add remaining ingredients and boil; reduce to a simmer. Taste to adjust seasonings after 20 to 30 minutes. Simmer for another 30 minutes. Serve with your favorite bread.

Serves 4-6

Kim Summers
Sarasota Waldorf School

Stone Soup

olive oil
onions, chopped
water
1 vegetable bouillon cube
vegetables brought by the children
2 small, round river stones

In the bottom of a soup pot, sauté the onions in olive oil. Add several inches of water to the pot and bring to a boil. Add the bouillon cube.

With the children's help, chop the vegetables. Add the vegetables to the pot, and add more water if necessary to cover the vegetables. Simmer until tender.

Just before serving, add the stones to the soup.

Serves 20-25 (the whole class!)

Lisa Hildreth – formerly of Green Meadow Waldorf School
Chestnut Ridge, NY

A Tale of the Stone Soup

Once there was an old man who had been traveling for a long time. He was poor and had no money or food. When he came to a village, he began to go from door to door to see if someone had food to spare. But wherever he went, the people said they had nothing to give and sent him away.

When he came to the last house, the man of the house jeered and said, "All I have to give you is water."

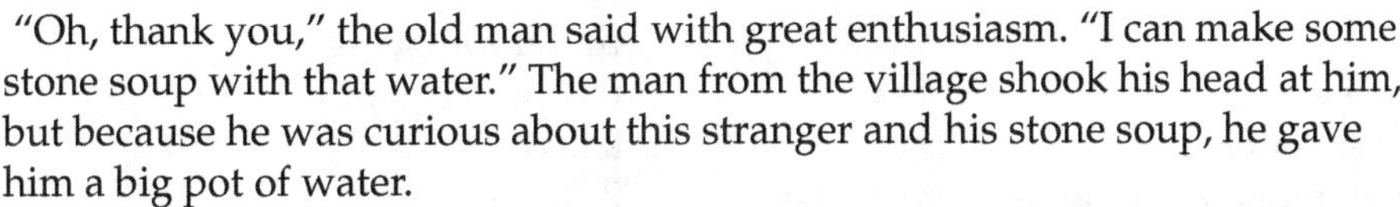

"Oh, thank you," the old man said with great enthusiasm. "I can make some stone soup with that water." The man from the village shook his head at him, but because he was curious about this stranger and his stone soup, he gave him a big pot of water.

The old man sang a merry tune as he built a small fire and set the pot upon it. He took a small, round stone out of his pocket and ceremoniously placed it in the pot. After a while a passerby stopped beside him and asked what he was doing there.

"Oh, I'm making stone soup. Would you like some when it's ready?"

"What does it taste like?" asked the villager.

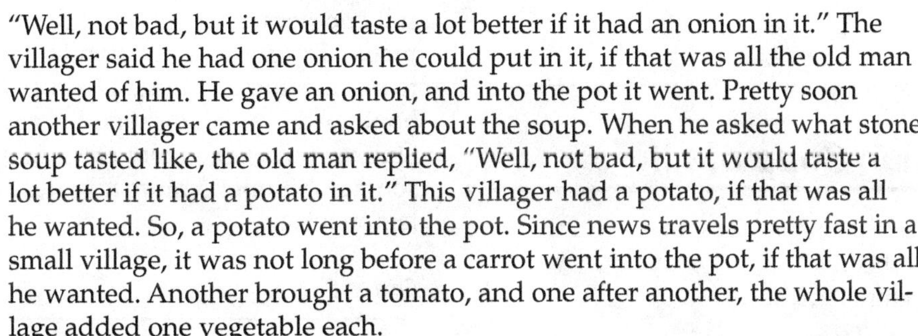

"Well, not bad, but it would taste a lot better if it had an onion in it." The villager said he had one onion he could put in it, if that was all the old man wanted of him. He gave an onion, and into the pot it went. Pretty soon another villager came and asked about the soup. When he asked what stone soup tasted like, the old man replied, "Well, not bad, but it would taste a lot better if it had a potato in it." This villager had a potato, if that was all he wanted. So, a potato went into the pot. Since news travels pretty fast in a small village, it was not long before a carrot went into the pot, if that was all he wanted. Another brought a tomato, and one after another, the whole village added one vegetable each.

Finally, when the soup was ready, the whole village was invited to eat. And eat they did – as much as they wanted. The old man, who had eaten his fill too, was careful, however, to retrieve the stone from the pot and put it back into his pocket for another day.

As retold by Marsha Post

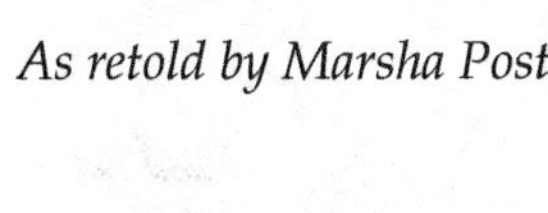

Beef Soups

Beef Barley Soup

1 cup whole barley (soaked overnight in 3 cups of water)
1 onion
1 carrot
2 cloves garlic
2 ribs celery
butter to sauté
5 cups beef stock
1 tsp. sea salt
1/2 tsp. pepper
dash of cayenne
chopped tomatoes or parsley for garnish

Cook soaked barley with a dash of sea salt. Reserve.

Sauté sliced vegetables in butter. Add to stock, and simmer. Add seasonings and barley. Simmer. Add more stock if necessary. Garnish and serve.

Serves 6

Russian Soup of Life

2 T. butter
1 onion, sliced
1 leek, white part, sliced
1 carrot, sliced
5 cups beef broth
3/4 pound cabbage, shredded
1/2 cup sauerkraut
1 tomato, peeled and cut into chunks
sea salt and pepper
sour cream
dill

Sauté vegetables in butter. Pour in stock. Bring to a boil. Stir in the shredded cabbage. Simmer covered for about 40 minutes. Add seasonings. Simmer for 10 more minutes. Garnish each serving with sour cream and dill.

Serves 6

Ox-Tail Soup

1 small ox-tail
flour for dredging
butter for frying
6 cups beef stock
2 carrots
2 turnips
1 onion
2 ribs celery
1/2 tsp. sea salt
dash cayenne pepper
1 tsp. Worcestershire Sauce
1 tsp. lemon juice

Cut ox-tail in small pieces, wash, drain. Add salt and pepper to flour and dredge ox-tail pieces. Fry in butter for 10 minutes. Add to stock. Simmer 1 hour. Drain and discard bones. Add ox-tail meat and vegetables. Simmer until vegetables are soft. Add seasonings. Simmer 5 more minutes and add lemon juice.

Serves 6

Chicken Soups

Egg and Lemon Chicken Soup

8 cups homemade or non-fat chicken stock
2 6-ounce boneless, skinless chicken breasts
1 carrot, peeled and cut into chunks
1 medium stalk celery, sliced
1 bay leaf
1 cup long-grain white rice
2 eggs
1 T. cold water
juice of 2 small lemons (about 1/2 cup)
salt and freshly ground black pepper, to taste

Place the stock, chicken breasts, carrot, celery, bay leaf and rice in a large pot. Cover and bring to a boil over high heat. Reduce the heat to low; keep covered. Stir occasionally and simmer for 30 minutes, or until the vegetables are tender and the rice is cooked al dente.

Remove the chicken breasts from the soup and slice into strips. Return strips to the broth. In a bowl, beat the eggs and water until the eggs are frothy. Spoon out the hot chicken broth and carefully add it to the egg mixture a few spoonfuls at a time, while continuously beating. When all the broth is incorporated, add the lemon juice and beat to blend. Pour the egg-lemon mixture back into the chicken soup pot, season with salt and pepper, and stir to blend well throughout. Remove the bay leaf and serve hot.

Serves 4

Linda Gambrell, Alumni Parent
Pleasant Ridge Waldorf School
Viroqua, WI

Hearty Chicken Noodle Soup for Crockery Slow Cooker

2 to 2-1/2 pounds chicken parts, skinned
6 cups water
1 medium onion, chopped
6 carrots, cut into 1/2-inch pieces
5 ribs celery, cut into 1/2-inch pieces
1 14-1/2 ounce can whole tomatoes, cut up, including liquid
1-1/2 T. instant chicken bouillon
1 T. dried parsley flakes
1 tsp. salt
1/2 tsp. dried rosemary leaves
1/2 tsp. pepper
1 cup uncooked fine egg noodles

Cook at: Low for 8-10 hours: High for 5-6 hours, or Auto for 6-7 hours.

Combine all ingredients, except egg noodles, in stoneware cooking pot. Place pot into heating base, cover and cook at desired heat setting for time given or until chicken and vegetables are tender. Remove chicken pieces from cooking pot and set aside to cool slightly. Set control to High and add noodles, stirring to combine. Cover and continue to cook 30 minutes. Meanwhile, remove chicken from bones and cut into bite-size pieces. Return meat to cooking pot and cook until noodles are tender. Set at Low for serving.

Serves 6-8

Sheila Grams, Parent
Pleasant Ridge Waldorf School
Viroqua, WI

Seafood Soups

Clam and Tomato Bisque

1 quart shucked clams
1-1/2 cups cold water or fish fumet
1 stick or 1/2 cup butter
1/3 cup flour
1 onion, chopped
2 cups cream
1 small can or 1 cup stewed tomatoes
sea salt
cayenne

Pour water over clams, then drain. Reserve liquid. To water, add hard parts of clams, finely chopped. Heat slowly to boiling point. Cook 20 minutes, then strain and reserve liquid. Sauté onion in butter for 5 minutes. Add flour and, gradually, clam water. Add cream, clams, and, as soon as boiling-point is reached, tomatoes. Season with salt and cayenne.

Serves 6

Charley's Chowder

3 6-ounce cans minced clams
3 6-1/2-ounce cans chopped clams
5 slices extra thick bacon, cut into 1 inch pieces
1 large onion, minced, but not too small pieces
3 T. flour
1 cup water
2 cup peeled raw potatoes, diced to 1-inch cubes
2 bay leaves
1 11-ounce can corn, drained
4 cups milk
3 T. butter

Drain clams and reserve clam juice. Combine with water and heat. Slowly sauté bacon. When crisp, remove with slotted spoon and set aside. Sauté onion in bacon drippings until translucent. Slowly sift flower into onions, blending well. Slowly stir in heated clam juice and water mixture. Add potatoes and bay leaves.

Cover and simmer until potatoes are just done but still firm. Add corn, bacon, milk, butter. Simmer about 5 minutes. Add dash white pepper. Serve with oyster crackers, warm baguette or other fresh bread. Some enjoy a chilled white wine accompaniment also.

Serves 8-10 (a half-recipe makes up nicely too). We have this once or twice a year, usually after the Advent Spiral Garden festival or on New Year's Eve.

Charley Canniff, Treasurer
Sarasota Waldorf School

Fish Chowder Home Style

We make this frequently, using fish we've caught locally. Our children love it and will eat several bowls.

For the fumet:

2-1/2 cups cold water
1/2 cup chopped onions
shallots
1/4 cup chopped carrots
1/2 cup chopped celery
6 white peppercorns
3-4 cloves
bouquet garnis
twist of lemon rind
1/2 cup dry white wine
2 T. lemon juice
1 to 1-1/2 pounds washed, lean fish bones: tails, shins, trimmings, and heads (no gills).

Fish heads are particularly flavorful, but avoid trimmings from strong-flavored fish like mackerel, skate or mullet. Use salmon only for salmon sauce. Shells from crab, shrimp, and lobster are delicious additions. Heat until the liquid begins to simmer, and continue simmering, uncovered, no longer than 15 minutes — or a bitter flavor may develop. Skim surface to remove scum. Add at last minute: any extra oyster or clam juice. Strain and use in soups or sauces.

For the Chowder:

2-1/2 pounds chopped, uncooked, boneless white-fleshed fish
5 cups fumet
sea salt and pepper
1/4 pound bacon
2 onions, finely chopped
2 cups uncooked potatoes, peeled and diced
1 cup milk, strained and scalded
1 cup heavy cream
pinch thyme
few grains nutmeg
1 T. parsley, finely chopped
1 T. butter
saltines

Fry bacon until nearly crisp. Remove some bacon fat and make a roux with it to thicken soup. Add onions, sauté until transparent. Wash fish. Heat fumet. Add bacon and onions. Add diced potatoes. Cook until potatoes are done. Add fish. Add milk, cream, thyme, parsley, sea salt, pepper, nutmeg

Heat through. Just before serving add butter and crushed saltines.

Serve in shallow bowls each containing a toasted cracker and a bit of minced parsley.

Serves 8-10

David Heath, Parent
Pleasant Ridge Waldorf School
Viroqua, WI

Lobster Bisque

2 pounds lobster
2 cups cold water
4 cups whole milk
1/2 cup butter
1/4 cup flour
1-1/2 t. salt
few grains cayenne

Remove meat from lobster shell. Chop meat and reserve.

Add cold water to shell and tough end of claws. Bring slowly to boiling point and cook twenty minutes. Drain, reserve liquor, and thicken with butter and flour cooked together. Scald milk with tail meat of lobster, finely chopped; strain and add to liquor. Season with salt and cayenne. Add tender claw meat, diced, and body meat.

When coral is found in lobster: wash, wipe, force through fine strainer, put into a food processor with butter and work until well blended, then add flour and stir into soup. If richer soup is desired, add rich chicken broth instead of water.

Serves 4-6

Bok Choy Shrimp Soup

Every few years our favorite recipes change — this is definitely the fave of the moment, simple and quick and surprisingly hearty.

1 T. vegetable oil (I use sesame oil)
1 10-1/2 ounce can chicken broth
1 cup shitake mushrooms, sliced
1/8 tsp. crushed red pepper flakes
1 baby bok choy, sliced (about 2 cups)
2 T. green onions, finely chopped
3 1/4-inch-thick slices ginger
6 ounces frozen raw baby shrimp
1 cup cooked rice
1 T. lime juice

Heat oil in medium pan. Add mushrooms, bok choy, and ginger. Sauté 5 minutes or until mushrooms are tender. Add broth and bring to boil. Reduce heat to low. Add red pepper flakes, green onions and shrimp. Simmer 7 minutes or until shrimp are cooked through. Stir in rice and heat 1 to 2 minutes. Add lime juice. Remove ginger slices (or not). Serve hot.

Serves 2

Karen Pfeiffer, Alumni Parent
Pleasant Ridge Waldorf School
Viroqua, WI

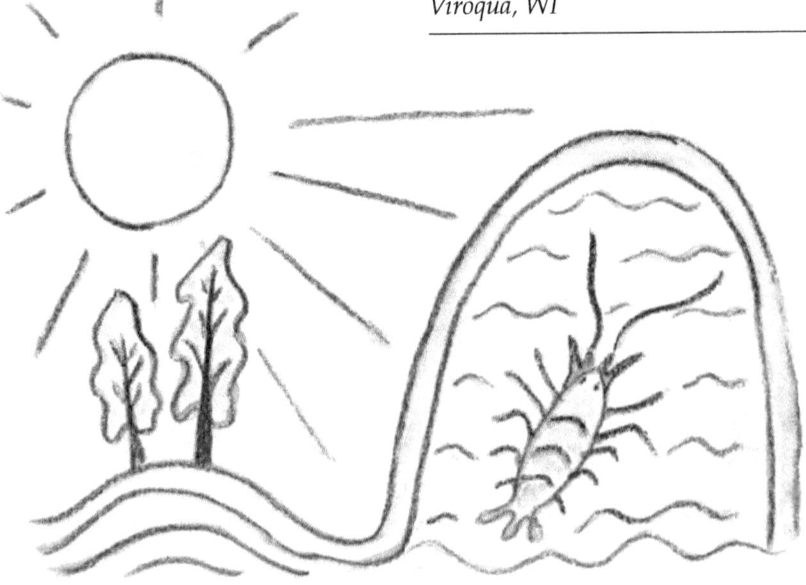

Creamy Corn Soup with Crabmeat and Egg

1 T. olive oil
1 13-ounce can creamed corn
sea salt and pepper
3 cloves garlic, crushed
1 T. Thai fish sauce
fresh cilantro, chopped
1 tsp. ginger, freshly grated
1 can (6 oz.) crab meat, drained
3 cups chicken stock
1 egg

Heat the oil in a large saucepan and cook garlic for one minute. Add ginger to the pan, then stir in the stock and the creamed corn, and bring to a boil. Stir in the fish sauce, crab meat, and salt and pepper. Return to boil. Beat the egg in a small bowl. Stir beaten egg into hot soup so it sets into long strands.

Garnish bowls of soup with cilantro.

Serves 4

Sheila Sherwin, Parent
Pleasant Ridge Waldorf School
Viroqua, WI

Oyster Stew

1 pint oysters, shucked
3 cups milk
butter
salt
pepper

Combine the oysters and some, but not all, of their packing liquid, add about 1/2 teaspoon salt and a little butter in a sauce pan. Cook on medium heat until the edges of the oysters curl. Add milk to cover the oysters and more butter. Heat through, but do not let it boil. Salt and pepper to taste.

Serve with crackers of your choice.

Serves 4

Velma Post
Rushville, Illinois

Hearty Soups

Gloria's Corn Chowder

5 cups water
2 onions, chopped
2 celery stalks, chopped
1 carrot, finely diced
2 or 3 large potatoes, diced
1 bay leaf
2 cups milk
10 ounces corn kernels (fresh or frozen)
sea salt and pepper to taste
parsley, finely chopped
paprika (as garnish)

Sauté onions in a little olive oil. Add water, celery, carrot, potatoes, and bay leaf. Bring to a boil, then simmer for about 20 minutes. Add corn, salt and pepper and simmer for another 5 minutes. Remove bay leaf. Add milk. Put about a third of the soup in a blender just long enough to form a creamy texture. Return the blended soup to the pan and stir well. Reheat, but do not let it boil. Serve with a sprinkle of paprika and parsley.

Serves 4-6

Gloria Kemp, Retired Teacher
Hawthorne Valley School
Ghent, NY

Chicken Chili

This is my favorite thing to make in the winter. I got the recipe from my aunt and have passed it along to many people.

1-1/4 pounds chicken, cut into bite-sized pieces
red onion, chopped
1 tsp. garlic
2 T. oil
15-ounce can kidney beans
15-ounce can pinto beans
24-ounce can chopped tomatoes
8-ounce can tomato sauce
1 tsp. pepper
1 tsp. red pepper flakes
1 tsp. salt
1 tsp. chili powder
2 T. Worcestershire sauce
1 tomato, diced
1 green, diced
3 to 4 mushrooms, diced
1 T. cornstarch, dissolved in 2 cups warm water

Combine chicken, onion, garlic, and oil in a big pot and cook until chicken is done. Add beans, tomatoes, and spices to pot. Bring to boil, simmer for 30 minutes. Add tomato, green pepper, mushrooms and cornstarch to pot. Cook on high for 5 minutes, stirring the entire time.

Serves 4 to 5

Paloma Shillings (Wright), Student from '85-'91
Pleasant Ridge Waldorf School
Viroqua, WI

"No one who cooks, cooks alone. Even at her most solitary, a cook in the kitchen is surrounded by generations of cooks past, the advice and menus of cooks present, the wisdom of cookbook writers."
— Laurie Colwin, American writer

Potato Leek Chowder

3 large leeks
5 red potatoes, peeled & quartered
1 T. butter or substitute
1 can chicken stock or equivalent vegetable stock
1 cup milk (or less, depending on if you like thick or thin soup)
1/2 cup plus grated cheddar cheese
sea salt and pepper

Wash leeks well and use only white bulbs and the upper, good portion of green stalks. Slice leeks. Peel and quarter potatoes. Melt butter in large stock pan and sauté leeks until a little tender, add potatoes and brown a little. Add stock and bring to boil, then lower heat, cover and simmer. When all is tender (15 minutes or so), add salt and pepper to taste and the milk and cheese and serve when hot.

Serves 4

Linda Finigan
Cape Ann Waldorf School
Beverly, MA

Harvest Stew

1 large pumpkin (round with a flat bottom)
3 T. butter
2 cloves garlic, minced
1 large onion, chopped
2 tomatoes, chopped
1 green pepper and 1/2 red pepper, diced
2 lbs turkey meat, diced
3 sweet potatoes, peeled and diced
3 jewel yams, peeled and diced
2 or 3 peaches, peeled and chopped (frozen will work)
4 ears corn, cut off cob
1-1/2 cups chicken broth
1 tsp. sugar
salt and pepper to taste

Fry garlic in butter, and afterward, discard the garlic. Add chopped onion and sauté a few minutes. Add tomatoes, peppers, turkey, salt, pepper, and sugar. Cook for 15 minutes, stirring occasionally. Add peaches and potatoes, and lower heat. Add corn and broth. Simmer 1 hour adding more broth (or dry red wine) if needed.

Meanwhile, back at the pumpkin patch, cut off top of pumpkin (jack-o'-lantern style). Remove seeds and membrane. Salt, pepper and butter the inside and rim (melted butter works best.) Bake at 350° F for 15 minutes with top on. Use a round shallow pan to support the pumpkin while baking. Remove from oven, fill with stew and return to oven for 15 to 20 minutes. When serving, scoop out the pumpkin with the stew.

Serves 6-8

I have made this stew for over 20 years. It was given to me by my best friend's (of over 30 years) mother, who is the best soup maker I've ever known. The original recipe called for ground beef, but I've always made it with turkey filet.

Donna Thomas, Class Rep Coordinator and Parent
Westside Waldorf School
Santa Monica, CA

Hearty Mushroom and Wild Rice Soup

2-1/2 T. butter
1-3/4 cups chopped onions
2 T. chopped fresh parsley
6 cups chicken stock or broth
3 T. wild rice
3-1/4 cups coarsely chopped fresh mushrooms (about 2/3 lb.)
2 T. long-grain white rice
1/4 tsp. dried thyme leaves
1/4 tsp. dried marjoram leaves
1/4 tsp. black pepper (preferably freshly ground)
1-1/2 T. tomato paste
1/4 cup water
1-2 tsp. finely chopped fresh chives for garnish (optional)

Combine the butter, onions, and parsley in a 3 to 4 quart pot. Cook over medium-high heat, stirring for 7 to 9 minutes, or until the onions are tender and golden but not browned; if necessary, lower the heat to prevent the onions from browning. Stir in the stock and wild rice and bring the mixture to a boil. Lower the heat and gently simmer the mixture, covered, for about 30 minutes.

Stir in the mushrooms, white rice, thyme, marjoram and pepper. Continue simmering the mixture, covered, for 15 to 20 minutes longer, or until the wild rice is cooked through but still slightly chewy.

In a small bowl, stir together the tomato paste and water until well blended; then add the mixture to the soup. Continue simmering for about 10 minutes longer. If desired, sprinkle the soup with chopped chives.

Serves 5-7

Leslie Burchell-Fox, Kindergarten Teacher
Green Meadow Waldorf School
Spring Valley, N.Y.

Baked Potato Soup

10 T. butter
2/3 cup flour
7 cup milk
6 potatoes baked, peeled, and cubed
4 green onions, chopped
1-1/4 cups cheddar cheese, shredded
1/2 cup sour cream
1/2 tsp. salt
1/2 tsp. pepper
6 strips bacon, crisply cooked and crumbled, *or* 1/4 cup imitation bacon bits

Melt the butter in a soup pot or Dutch oven. Add the flour and whisk until completely smooth. Over medium heat, pour in the milk, stirring constantly, until thickened. Add potatoes and onions. Continue to stir constantly until the soup returns to a boil. Reduce heat and simmer for 10 minutes. Add remaining ingredients, stirring until the cheese is melted.

Serves 6 to 8

Kathy Rinde, Kindergarten Teacher
Pasadena Waldorf School
Altadena, California

Yellow Potato-Leek Soup

3 celery stalks, sliced
1 medium white onions, thinly sliced
2 medium leeks, sliced then rinsed
3 garlic cloves, sliced
2 T. olive oil
3 medium yellow Finn potatoes, cut into uniform chunks
3 large red potatoes, cut into uniform chunks
pinch fresh parsley
2 tsp. cumin
2 tsp. basil
2 bay leaves
3 T. soy sauce
1/2 tsp. black pepper
pinch chopped dill

Sauté celery, onion, leeks, and garlic in oil for 2 to 3 minutes. Combine all ingredients (except dill) in stockpot and cover with water. Simmer for 30 to 45 minutes, until potatoes are soft. Reserving 1/2 to 1 cup vegetables, blend soup into a puree using a blender, food processor or potato ricer.

Combine fresh dill and reserved vegetables with puree. Reheat and serve.

Serves 6

Ruth Col, Parent
Waldorf School of San Diego

Harvest Soup

5-6 lbs. winter squash (hubbard, acorn, butternut, etc.)
1 can coconut milk
4 T. butter
1 cup onion, diced
2 T. fresh ginger, peeled and grated
1 tsp. cinnamon
1 tsp. curry powder
1/2 tsp. each allspice and nutmeg
2 tsp. sea salt, or to taste
(garam masala and pumpkin pie spice have also been used with success)

Bake squash, allow to cool and then scoop into blender. Puree until smooth, and add coconut milk slowly while blending. This may be done in batches. In pot, simmer onion in butter. Add squash puree and spices. Simmer slowly for awhile — the longer the yummier. If thinner soup is preferred, vegetable or chicken broth can be added.

Serves 8-10

Gloria S. Leon, 6th-Grade Teacher
Washington Waldorf School
Bethesda, Marylan

Chilled Soups

Avocado, Lime, and Cilantro Soup

2 ripe avocados
2 T. fresh lime juice
2 T. sour cream or créme fraiche
1 small mild onion, chopped
3 cups vegetable stock
1 clove garlic, crushed
1 T. rice vinegar
1 T. cilantro
2 T. cilantro, chopped
1 T. soy sauce
2 T. lime juice
1 T. fresh mint, chopped
salt and pepper
fine shreds of lime rind

Halve, pit, and scoop out the flesh from the avocados. Place in a blender or food processor with onion, garlic, cilantro, mint, lime juice, and approximately 1/2 of the stock. Process until smooth. Add the remaining stock, rice wine vinegar, and soy sauce and blend again. Taste and adjust for seasoning, adding more lime juice or salt and pepper. Cover and chill.

Lime-Cream Garnish:
Mix together lime, cilantro, and sour cream (or créme fraiche). Spoon into the soup just before serving and sprinkle with lime rind.

Serves 4

Sheila Sherwin, Parent
Pleasant Ridge Waldorf School
Viroqua, WI

Beet and Celery Soup

1 cup onions, chopped
2 cups celery, sliced
1/4 cup butter
sea salt and black pepper
4-5 beets, boiled, peeled and cubed
1 T. ume plum vinegar (Asian plum vinegar) *or* 1 T. red wine vinegar, plus additional to taste
3 cups chicken broth
ice water for thinning soup

Garnish: sour cream with horseradish and minced chives

Sauté onion and celery with butter. Add salt and pepper. Stir until vegetables are softened. Add beets, vinegar, and broth and simmer about twenty minutes. Puree in food processor or blender in batches, until smooth. Transfer to bowl, and chill, covered. When ready to serve, thin soup with ice water and check for seasonings. Garnish with sour cream and chives.

Serves 4

Curry Soup

2 cups rich chicken stock
2 tsp. curry powder
1 tsp. lemon juice
2 egg yolks
1/2 cup heavy cream
scallions, thinly sliced on the diagonal

Season 2 cups of rich chicken stock with curry powder and lemon juice. Heat to a simmer. Beat 2 egg yolks into heavy cream, and add some heated broth. Gradually add egg and cream to rest of broth. Simmer for about 5 minutes. Chill. Garnish at serving time with scallions.

Serves 2

Coconut Carrot Soup with Curry

1 bunch scallions, sliced thinly on the diagonal
1 onion, chopped
1/4 cup butter
4 cups carrots, sliced
sea salt and white pepper
1 T. curry powder
3 cups chicken broth
1-1/2 cups canned coconut milk
1 T. lime juice
Fresh ginger juice, squeezed from peeled, grated, fresh ginger root *or* 1 tsp. dried ginger powder
chives for garnish

In a large heavy pot sauté scallions and onion in butter with curry powder. Add salt and pepper, and carrots. Sauté over moderately low heat. Add broth and simmer about 20 minutes, until carrots are soft. Add coconut milk. Heat through. Puree in food processor, or blender. Stir in lime juice and ginger. Chill several hours or overnight. Thin soup if necessary with ice water, or chicken broth. Check for seasoning. Garnish with chopped chives.

Serves 6-8

Vichyssoise (Leek and Potato Soup)

4 medium-sized leeks, white part only
1 medium-sized onion
1/2 cup butter
5 medium-sized potatoes, peeled and finely sliced
4 cups chicken broth
1-2 cups heavy cream
sea salt and white pepper
chopped watercress, parsley, or chives

Sauté leeks and onions in butter. Add potatoes. Add chicken broth, and sea salt and white pepper. Simmer until vegetables are tender.

Cool. Process in blender or food processor until smooth. Add cream. Chill.

Serve with garnish of watercress, parsley, or chives.

Serves 4

Dessert Soups

Cherry Soup

2 pounds cherries, pitted, or 2 10-ounce bags frozen, pitted cherries
2 cups water
cinnamon stick
2 cloves
2 drops almond extract (optional)
1/4 tsp. sea salt
2 cups red wine (Cabernet or California Claret)
1 T. brandy
agave syrup or dried sugar cane juice
2 egg yolks

Put cherries in a large, non-reactive, (preferably enamel) thick-bottomed pot. Add water, cinnamon stick, cloves, almond extract, and salt. Process in a blender, food processor, or food mill, until smooth. Return to pot; add wine, brandy and sweetener to taste. Whisk in beaten egg yolks, and cook until slightly thick.

Serve well chilled.

Serves 4

Fruit Soup

1-3/4 quarts water
7/8 cup sugar
1/2 vanilla bean
3 limes
1 large orange
3 cups mixed fruit, chopped

Combine the water and sugar in a pot. Scrape the inside of the bean and add the scrapings and the bean to the pot. Zest and juice the limes and orange and add to the pot. Bring everything to a boil. Remove from heat. Let cool, strain, then refrigerate before serving.

Up to an hour before serving, add approximately 3 cups mixed fruit, such as apples, strawberries, pineapple, grapes.

Garnish with fresh mint or lemon basil.

Serves approximately 8

Nicole Persson, 2nd-Year Student of the Bay Area Center for Waldorf Teacher Training & Business Manager, Marin Waldorf School

Kaernemaeiks Suppe (Danish Buttermilk Soup)

My second-generation, Danish-American roommates and I enjoyed celebrating on a Saturday or Sunday around the summer solstice time with a brunch on the front porch. We served "Kaernemaeiks Suppe" in our fanciest creamed soup cups with silver creamed soup spoons, lace table cloth, and all. Brunch was followed by the telling of "The Three Billy Goats Gruff," in Danish. A rich event from all perspectives.

Beat together:
3 eggs
1/4 frozen orange juice concentrate
juice of one lemon

Heat 1 qt. butter milk to just boiling. Slowly add the egg mixture. Heat, but do not boil. Do not overcook.

Top each serving with a dollop of unsweetened whipped cream.

Serves 4

Diane Canniti, Playgroup Leader
Sarasota Waldorf School

Apricot Soup

1 pound apricots + 4 nice apricots
2 cups water
2 T. breadcrumbs
2 glasses + 1 T. white wine
1 T. honey
3 egg yolks

Scald, peel, and pit the pound of apricots. Combine the apricots, breadcrumbs, and water, and cook until soft. Add the 2 glasses of wine and bring to a boil. Remove from heat and let it cool down. Stir in the honey and egg yolks; heat until the mixture is thick.

Halve and pit the 4 nice apricots. Place them with the tablespoon of white wine in a covered (fireproof) baking dish and bake until the apricots are soft. Place these apricots in the bottom of a soup tureen and pour the soup over them.

This soup can be served hot or cold and is especially delicious accompanied by macaroons.

Serves 4

Anonymous

Big Soups

Big Soup

1 stick butter
3 onions, chopped
3 ribs celery, sliced
6 large carrots, sliced on the diagonal
4 cloves garlic
6-8 cups split peas, brown lentil, *or*
red lentils, sorted, rinsed and drained
4 quarts water, brought to a rolling boil
sea salt
tamari
tomato paste
1/2 tsp. thyme
1/2 tsp. oregano
1 bay leaf
grated cheese for garnish

Heat large pot of water. Sauté vegetables until tender. Add the small beans to boiling water. Add vegetables and seasoning, except for salt. Reduce temperature, and simmer until beans are tender, stirring often. Add sea salt. Check for seasonings. Add more butter, or olive oil, if more richness is called for.

Serves 10-12

Shani Williams, Head Teacher
Sheltering Arms Family Center
(Waldorf Early Childhood and Parent Education Programs)
Kimberton, PA

Vegetarian Chili

3 ounces prepared salsa
1/2 lb. dried kidney beans
1/2 lb. dried black beans
1 cup lentils
2-3 medium onions, diced
6 mediun garlic cloves, diced
2 stalks celery, sliced
1 green pepper, diced
4 plum tomatoes, diced
1 can Rotel brand tomatoes and green chilies
3 ounces olives oil
1 24-ounce can crushed tomatoes
1/4 cup molasses or maple syrup
1/2 tsp. dry mustard
2 T. dried basil
2 T. dried oregano
sea salt and pepper
1 tsp. cilantro
1 cup bulgur wheat, precooked in 2 cups boiling water with a pinch of sea salt

Sort, rinse, and soak dried beans (lentils need not be pre-soaked) for 24 hours. Drain. Put soaked beans and lentils in large pot. Cover with water and cook on low temperature until tender, about 2 hours. When beans are about 70% cooked, add sea salt.

While beans are cooking, prepare bulgur wheat. Reserve.

Sauté garlic, onions, celery, and green pepper until tender. When beans are tender, add sautéed vegetables and remainder of vegetables to the pot. Add more water if necessary. Cook on low temperature, skimming off "scum." Add pre-cooked bulgur wheat. Add more water if necessary. Heat through. Serve over brown rice, or in taco shells with cheese.

Serves 18 (one cup portions).

Leslie Burchell-Fox, Kindergarten Teacher
Green Meadow Waldorf School
Spring Valley, NY

Notes

Notes

About the Editor

Andrea Huff was born and raised in Norristown, Pennsylvania. She studied cooking in Boston, Massachusetts, in the mid 1970s and received a B.A in Early Childhood Education from Antioch University. She is a graduate of the Spatial Dynamics Institute and a student of Anthroposophy. In 1991, at the Kimberton Waldorf School, Andrea founded one of the first organic food school lunch programs in the United States. She managed that program, known as "Lunch at the Waldorf," for four years, until 1995. Andrea has been an organic and biodynamic foods caterer since 1991 and has worked as a personal chef since 2001.

About the Illustrator

Jo Valens teaches in the kindergarten at the Rudolf Steiner School in Great Barrington, Massachusetts. She lives with her husband Michael. They are the parents of a grown son. Aside from her work, Jo enjoys drawing, gardening and good conversation.

Index